hello WINTER

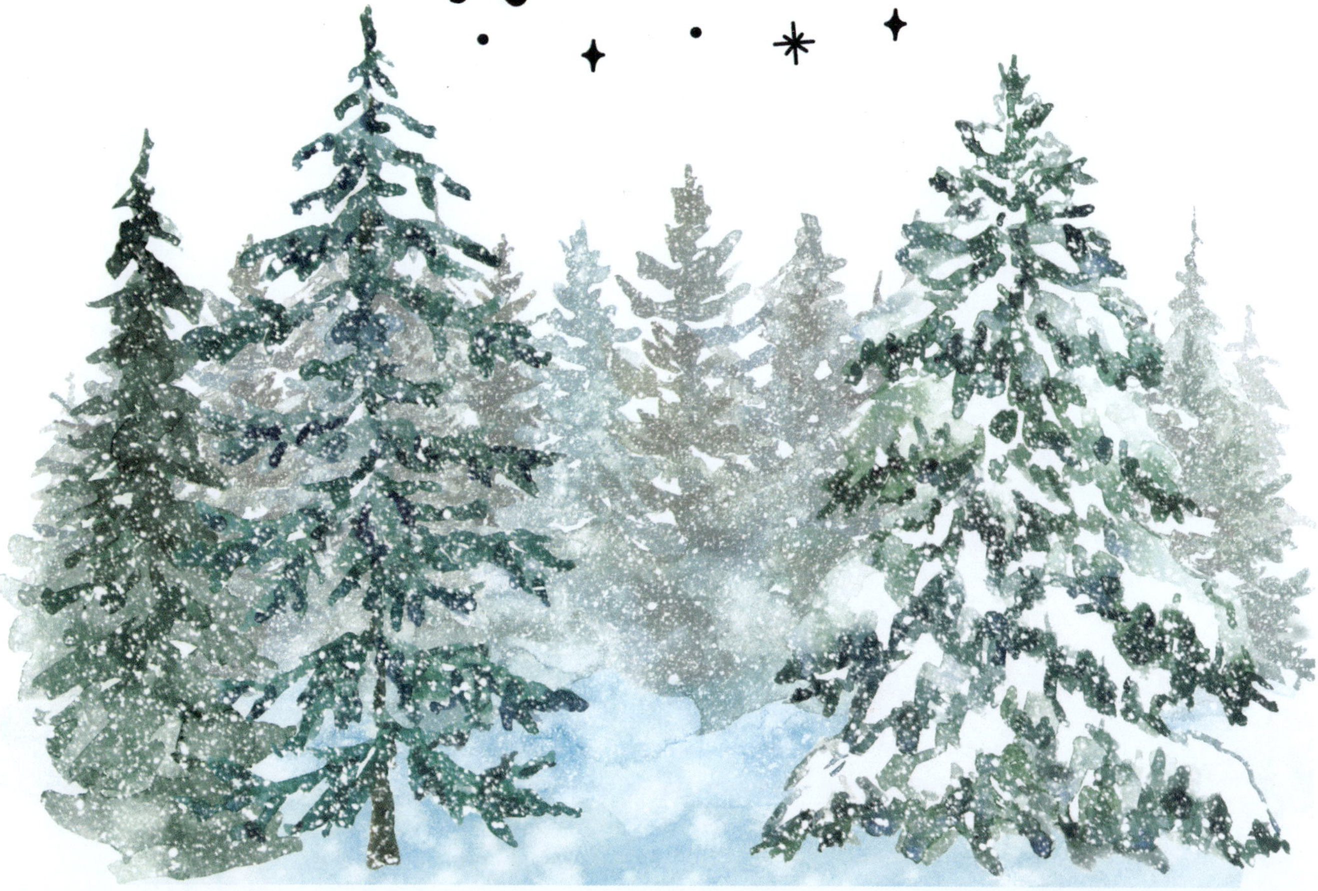

Welcome to Winter glow

A WINTER WELLNESS JOURNAL

Winter is a season of stillness, reflection, and renewal. This journal is designed to help you embrace the magic of winter, cultivate gratitude, and nurture your well-being. Through simple plant-based recipes, mindfulness activities, nature connections, and creative crafts, you'll find warmth and inspiration in every page. Use this journal as a companion to guide you through the winter months, inviting you to slow down, reflect, and connect with the beauty of the season.

Let's
GLOW!

WHAT IS WELLNESS

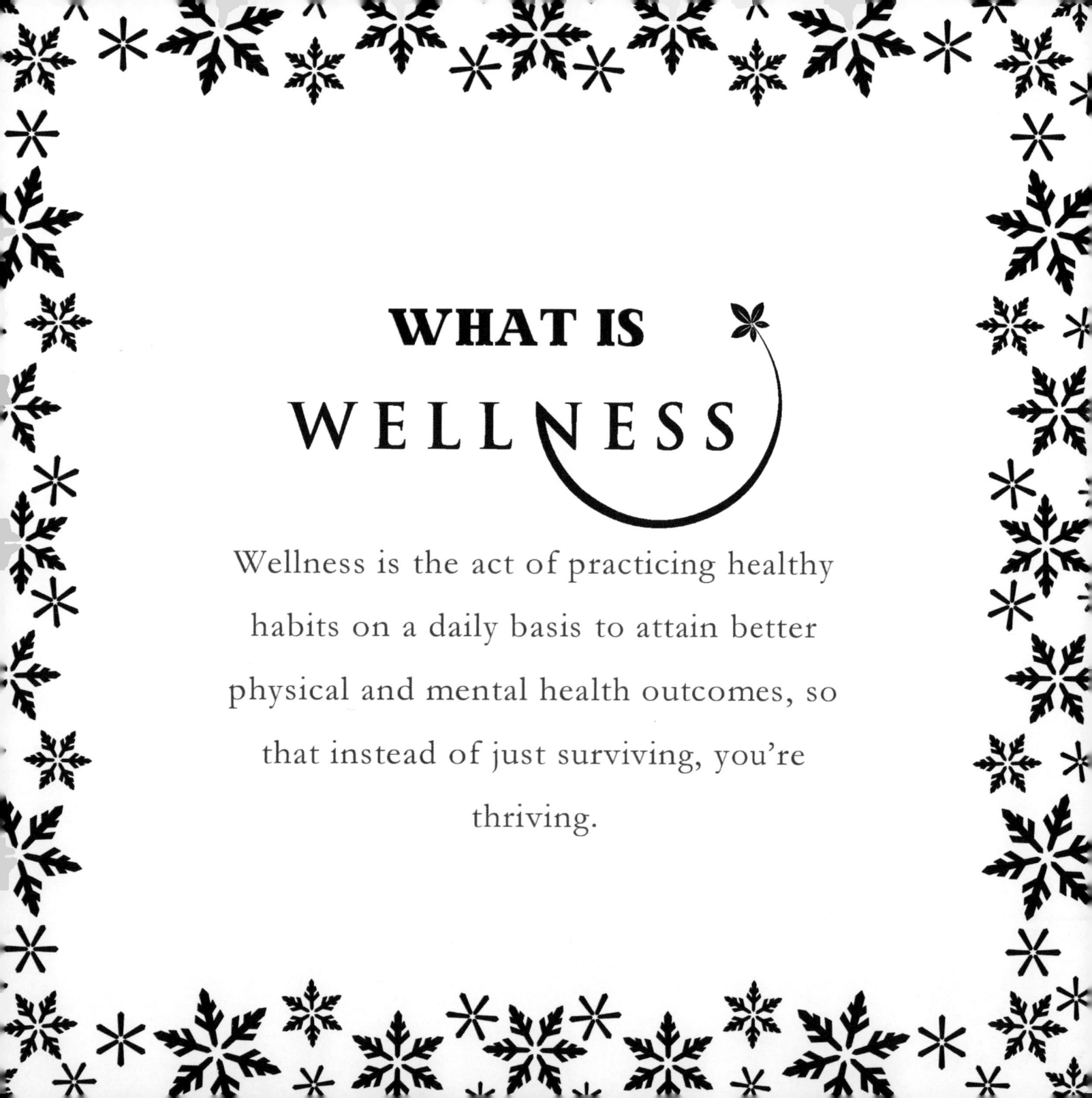

Wellness is the act of practicing healthy habits on a daily basis to attain better physical and mental health outcomes, so that instead of just surviving, you're thriving.

HOW TO USE THIS JOURNAL

Daily Reflections: Start each day with a gratitude prompt and a mindfulness activity to set a positive tone.

Weekly Invitations: Explore simple plant-based recipes, nature-inspired crafts, and wellness tips to enhance your well-being.

Monthly Highlights: Celebrate the unique aspects of each winter month with special activities and reflections.

Seasonal Celebrations: Embrace the magic of winter solstice and other seasonal events with guided meditations and rituals.

Winter Letter to Myself

Dear . . . .
As the winter season envelops us in its serene embrace,
 I take this moment to reflect on the past year and set intentions for the months ahead. Winter is a time of stillness, introspection, and renewal. It offers a unique opportunity to slow down, appreciate the beauty around us, and nurture our inner selves.
In this letter, I want to acknowledge my achievements, challenges, and growth.
 I am proud of the progress I have made and the resilience I have shown. I am grateful for the lessons learned and the experiences that have shaped me.
As I look forward to the coming months, I set intentions to embrace the magic of winter. I will find joy in the simple pleasures, such as a warm cup of tea, a cosy blanket, and the beauty of a snowy landscape. I will take time for self-care, mindfulness, and creativity. I will connect with nature, even in the coldest days,
 and find inspiration in its quiet strength.
I remind myself to be kind and gentle with myself, to celebrate my successes, and to learn from my setbacks. I will cherish the moments of stillness and use them to recharge and reflect. I will nurture my relationships and spread warmth and kindness to those around me.
Winter is a season of transformation, and I am ready to embrace it with an open heart and a positive spirit. I look forward to the growth, joy, and magic that this season will bring.
With love and warmth,
 X

Mindfulness Activity:

Take a few moments to sit quietly and focus on your breath. Imagine the warmth of a cosy fireplace enveloping you, bringing a sense of calm and peace.

Daily Reflection:
Today, I am grateful for..

Nature Connection:

Go for a winter walk and collect natural items like pine cones or evergreen sprigs. Create a small nature-inspired decoration for your home.

Daily Reflection:
Today, I am grateful for...

Creative Craft:

DIY Scented Candles

Materials: Soy wax, essential oils, candle wicks, and jars. Instructions: Melt the wax, add essential oils, place the wick in the jar, pour the wax, and let it cool.

Daily Reflection:
Today, I am grateful for...

The Winter Walk

One winter morning, Sarah decided to take a walk in the nearby forest to clear her mind. She had been feeling overwhelmed by work and personal challenges. As she walked through the snow-covered trees, she noticed the stillness and beauty of the winter landscape. The crisp air and the sound of crunching snow under her boots brought a sense of calm and clarity.

During her walk, Sarah encountered an elderly man named Thomas, who was also enjoying the winter scenery.

They struck up a conversation, and Thomas shared his wisdom about finding peace and balance in life. He spoke about the importance of taking time for oneself, embracing the present moment, and finding joy in simple pleasures. Inspired by their conversation, Sarah returned home with a renewed sense of purpose and a commitment to incorporating mindfulness and self-care into her daily routine.

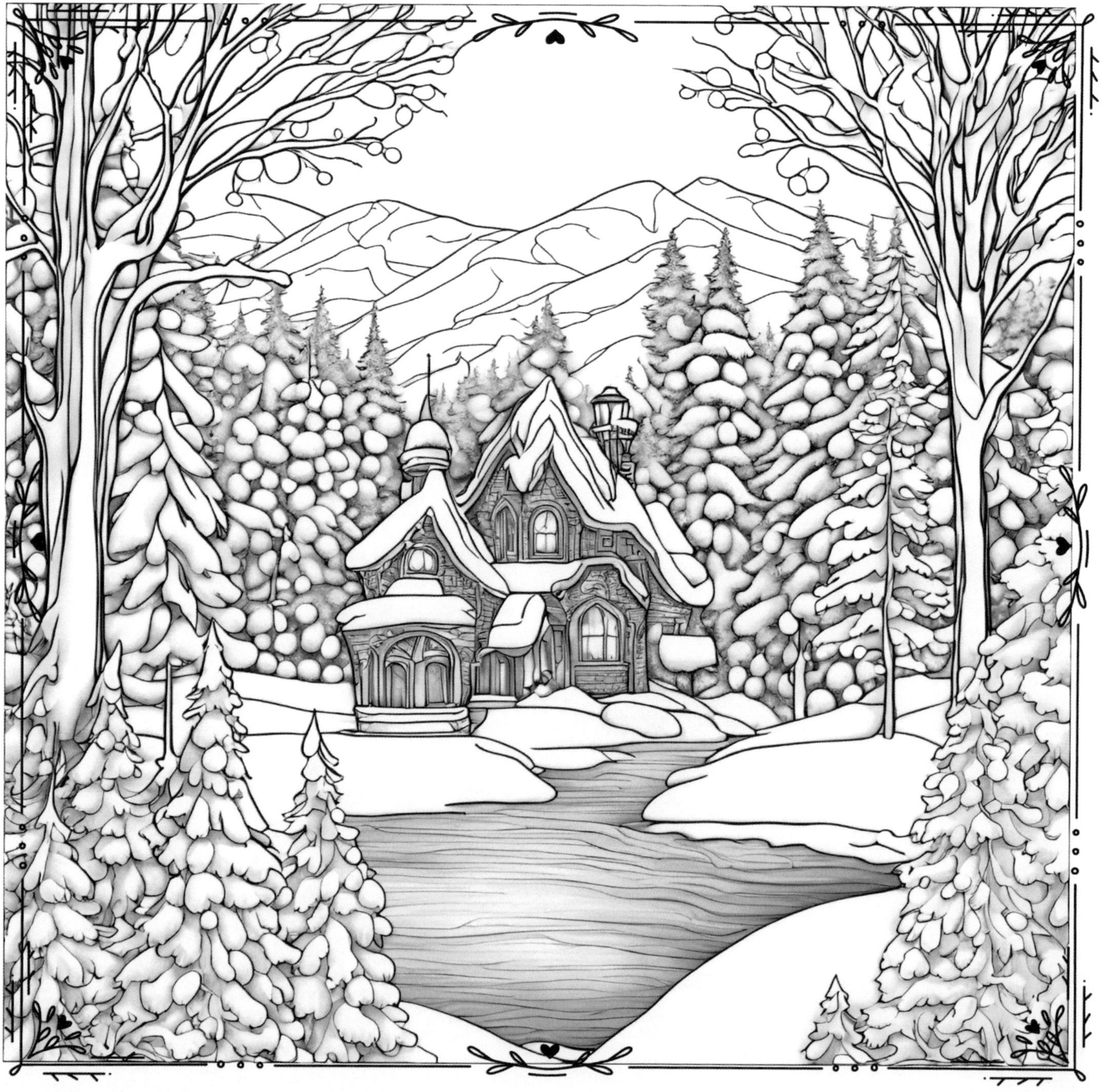

Simple Plant-Based Recipe:
Spiced Tea

Ingredients: Black tea, cinnamon sticks, cloves, cardamom pods, ginger, star anise and plant-based milk.
Directions: Brew the tea with spices, add plant-based milk, and enjoy a warm, comforting drink.

Daily Reflection:
Today, I am grateful for...

Nature Connection:

Spend some time observing the winter birds.
Notice their colours, behaviours, and sounds.
Reflect on the beauty and resilience of nature.

Daily Reflection:

Today, I am grateful for..

Mindfulness Activity:

Practice a few minutes of mindful stretching. Focus on the sensations in your body as you gently stretch and release tension. Imagine each stretch bringing warmth and relaxation.

Daily Reflection:

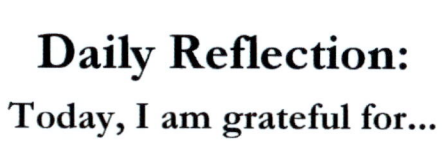

Today, I am grateful for...

Creative Craft:
DIY Winter Wreath

♡

Materials: Evergreen branches, pine cones, berries, and a wreath frame.
Instructions: Arrange the branches, pine cones, and berries on the wreath frame. Secure them with wire or string. Hang your wreath on your door or wall.

Daily Reflection:
Today, I am grateful for..

WINTER

TIP

Eat nutritious meals

Make the most of abundant winter root vegetables which are full of nutrients and so much goodness.

Roasted Root Vegetable Medley Recipe

Title: Roasted Root Vegetable Medley Ingredients:

2 large carrots, peeled and chopped

2 parsnips, peeled and chopped

1 sweet potato, peeled and chopped

1 beet, peeled and chopped

2 tablespoons olive oil

1 teaspoon dried thyme

1 teaspoon dried rosemary

Directions:

Preheat the oven to 400°F (200°C).

In a large bowl, toss the chopped root vegetables with olive oil, thyme, rosemary, salt, and pepper.

Spread the vegetables evenly on a baking sheet.

Roast in the preheated oven for 25-30 minutes, or until the vegetables are tender and golden brown.

Serve warm and enjoy the comforting flavours of winter.

The Spirit of Giving

Reflect on the spirit of giving and kindness.
Write down three acts of kindness you can
do for others this winter season.

Activity:

Create a small gift or treat for
someone special.
It could be a homemade cookie,
a handwritten note, or a small craft.
Spread the joy of giving by sharing
your creation.

Daily Reflection:
Today, I am grateful for...

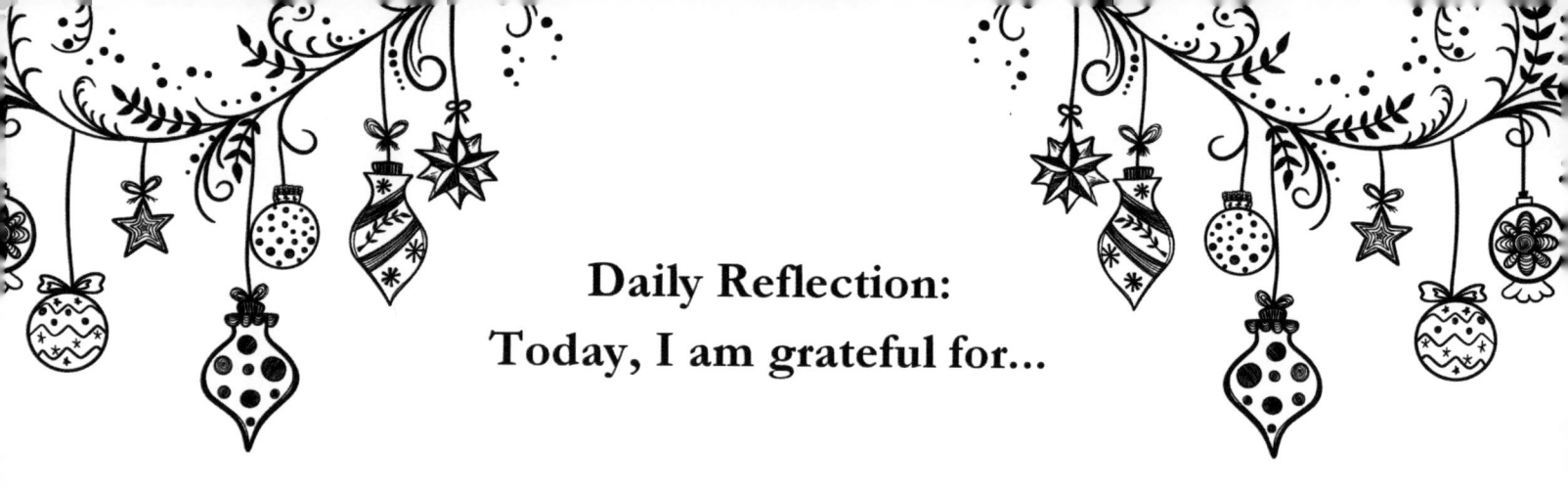

Nature Connection:
Spend some time observing the winter sky.
Notice the patterns of the clouds, the colours of the sunset,
and the twinkling stars. Reflect on the beauty of the season.

Magical Winter Playlist

Scan the QR code below to listen to a curated playlist of soothing and uplifting winter-themed music. Enjoy the magical sounds of the season as you journal and reflect.

[Insert QR Code Here]

Daily Reflection:
Today, I am grateful for...

Spiced Hot Cocoa

Ingredients: Cocoa powder, cinnamon, nutmeg, plant-based milk, and sweetener of choice.

Directions: Mix cocoa powder with spices, add plant-based milk, and sweeten to taste. Heat and enjoy a warm, comforting drink.

Daily Reflection:

Today, I am grateful for...

Self-Care

Self-care refers to practices that promote physical, mental, and emotional well-being, and enhance overall quality of life.

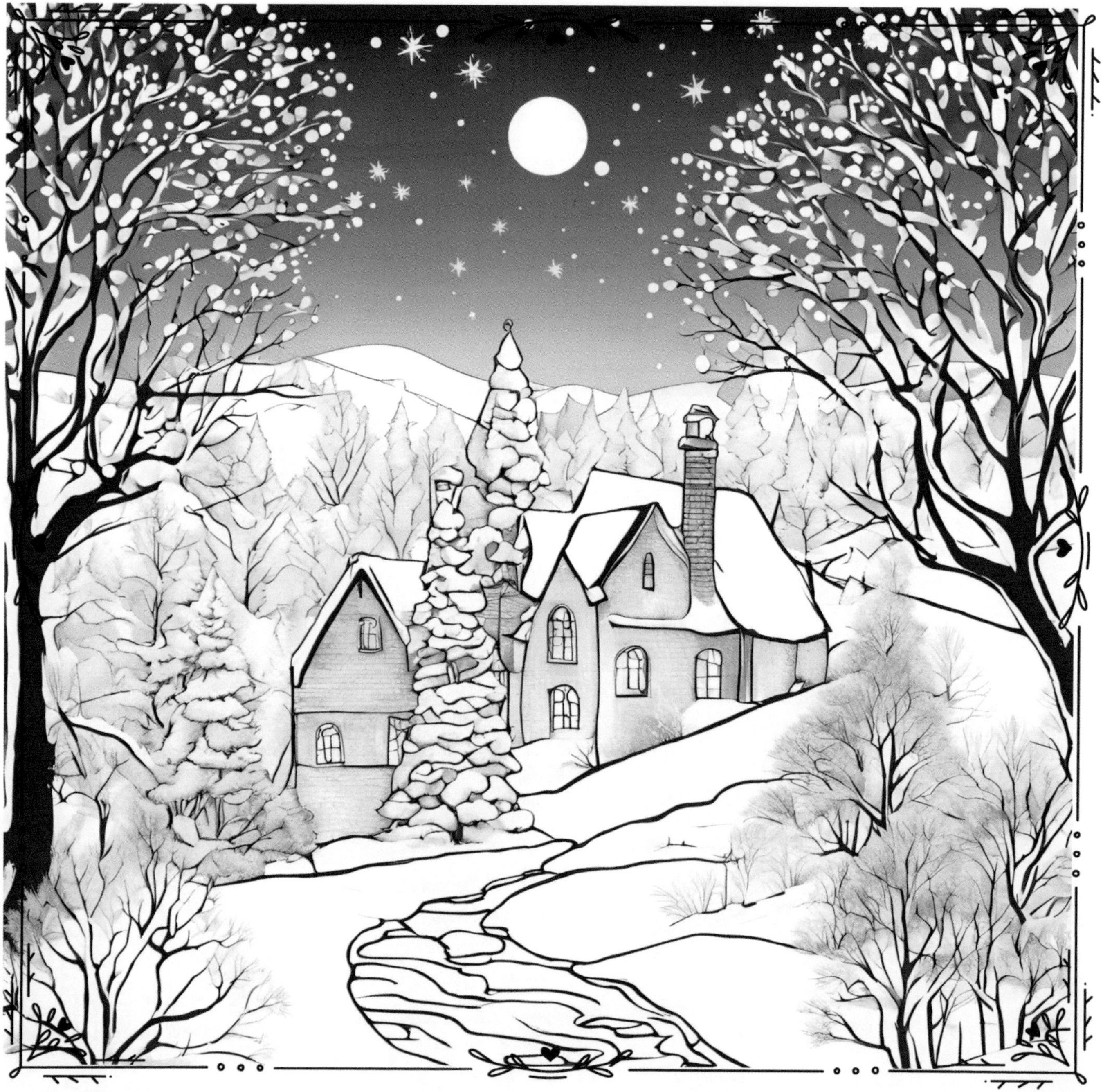

Mindful Activity:

Lie down in a comfortable position. Close your eyes and take a few deep breaths. Slowly scan your body from head to toe, noticing any areas of tension or discomfort. Breathe into those areas and release the tension.

Daily Reflection:

Today, I am grateful for...

Mindfulness Activity:

Light a candle and sit quietly for a few minutes. Focus on the flickering flame and let your mind relax. Reflect on the warmth and light the candle brings.

Daily Reflection:
Today, I am grateful for...

The Winter Garden

In a quiet town, there lived a woman named Clara who had always loved gardening. However, winter was a challenging time for her, as the cold weather made it difficult to tend to her beloved plants. One year, determined to keep her passion alive, Clara decided to create a winter garden in her home.

She started by researching indoor plants that thrived in winter conditions. With care and dedication, Clara transformed a corner of her living room into a lush, green sanctuary. She filled it with potted herbs, succulents, and even a small lemon tree. The sight of her winter garden brought her immense joy and a sense of accomplishment.

As the days grew shorter and colder, Clara found solace in her indoor oasis. She spent time each day tending to her plants, watering them, and ensuring they received enough light. The act of nurturing her winter garden became a form of meditation, helping her stay grounded and connected to nature.

One evening, Clara invited her neighbour, Mrs. Thompson, over for tea. Mrs. Thompson had recently lost her husband and was struggling with loneliness. When she saw Clara's winter garden, her eyes lit up with wonder. Clara shared the story of how she created the garden and offered to help Mrs. Thompson start her own.

continued ...

Together, they visited a local nursery and selected a variety of plants that would thrive indoors. Over the next few weeks, Clara and her neighbour worked side by side, transforming a corner of Mrs. Thompson's home into a beautiful winter garden. The project brought them closer together and provided a sense of purpose and companionship.

As winter progressed, Clara and Mrs. Thompson continued to nurture their gardens and their friendship. They exchanged tips, shared stories, and found joy in the simple act of caring for their plants. The winter gardens became a symbol of resilience and hope, reminding them that even in the coldest months, life could flourish.

Through her winter garden, Clara discovered the power of nature to heal and connect. She realised that the beauty of winter wasn't just in the snow-covered landscapes outside but also in the warmth and growth she cultivated within her home. The experience taught her that with a little creativity and determination, she could find joy and inspiration in any season.

Winter Bird feeder

Materials: Pine cones, peanut butter, birdseed, and string.

Instructions: Spread peanut butter on the pine cone, then roll it in birdseed. Tie a string around the top and hang it outside for the birds.

Daily Reflection:

Today, I am grateful for..

Winter Soup

Ingredients: Carrots, potatoes, celery, onions, garlic, vegetable broth, and herbs.

Directions: Sauté the onions and garlic, then add the chopped vegetables and broth. Simmer until the vegetables are tender. Season with herbs and enjoy a warm, comforting soup.

Daily Reflection:

Today, I am grateful for...

WINTER
TIP

Hydrate your skin

Keep dryness away and use heavier moisturisers in the cooler months.

INFUSED WATER

Benefits For Your Body.

Detoxification
Aids in detoxification and enhances the body's natural mechanisms.

Antioxidant Intake
Supplies antioxidants to fight radicals and inflammation.

Energy Boost
Natural sugars found in fruits provide a mild energy boost without the risk of caffeine crashes.

Creative Craft:
Winter Potpourri

Materials: Dried orange slices, cinnamon sticks, cloves, star anise and pine cones.

Instructions: Mix all the ingredients in a bowl and place them in a decorative jar. You could also add a few drops of frankincense essential oil to the winter mix, Enjoy the natural winter scent.

Daily Reflection:
Today, I am grateful for..

Festive Traditions

Reflect on your favourite festive traditions and memories. Write down the joy and warmth of spending time with loved ones.

Activity:
Create a cosy atmosphere by lighting candles, playing festive music, and enjoying a warm drink. Spend time with family and friends, sharing stories and laughter.

Daily Reflection:

Today, I am grateful for...

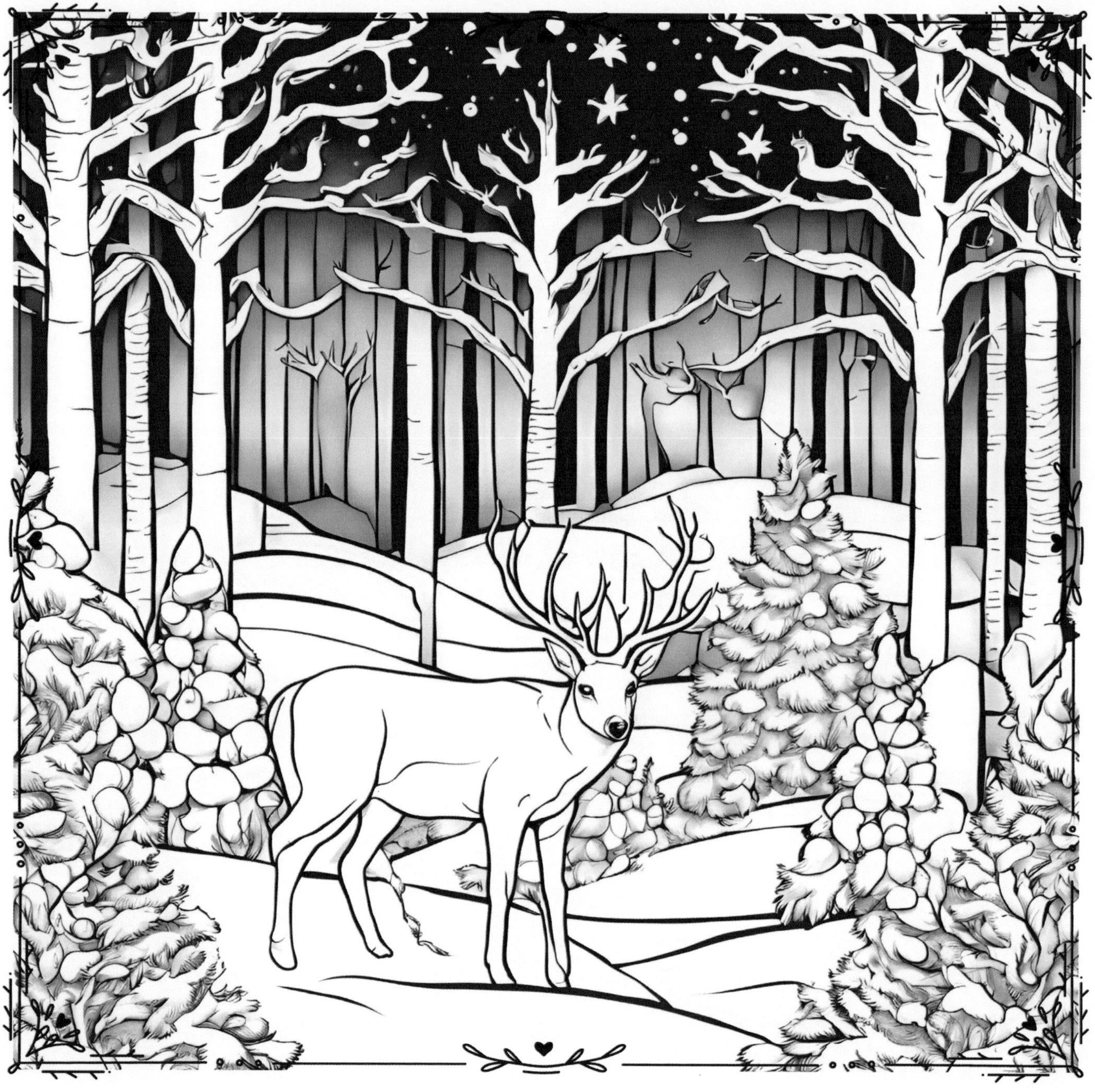

Daily Reflection:

Today, I am grateful for...

Creative Craft:

Materials: Cardstock, markers, stickers, and decorative paper.

Instructions: Fold the cardstock in half to create a card. Decorate the front with markers, stickers, and decorative paper. Write a heartfelt message inside and send them by post.

Mindful Activity:

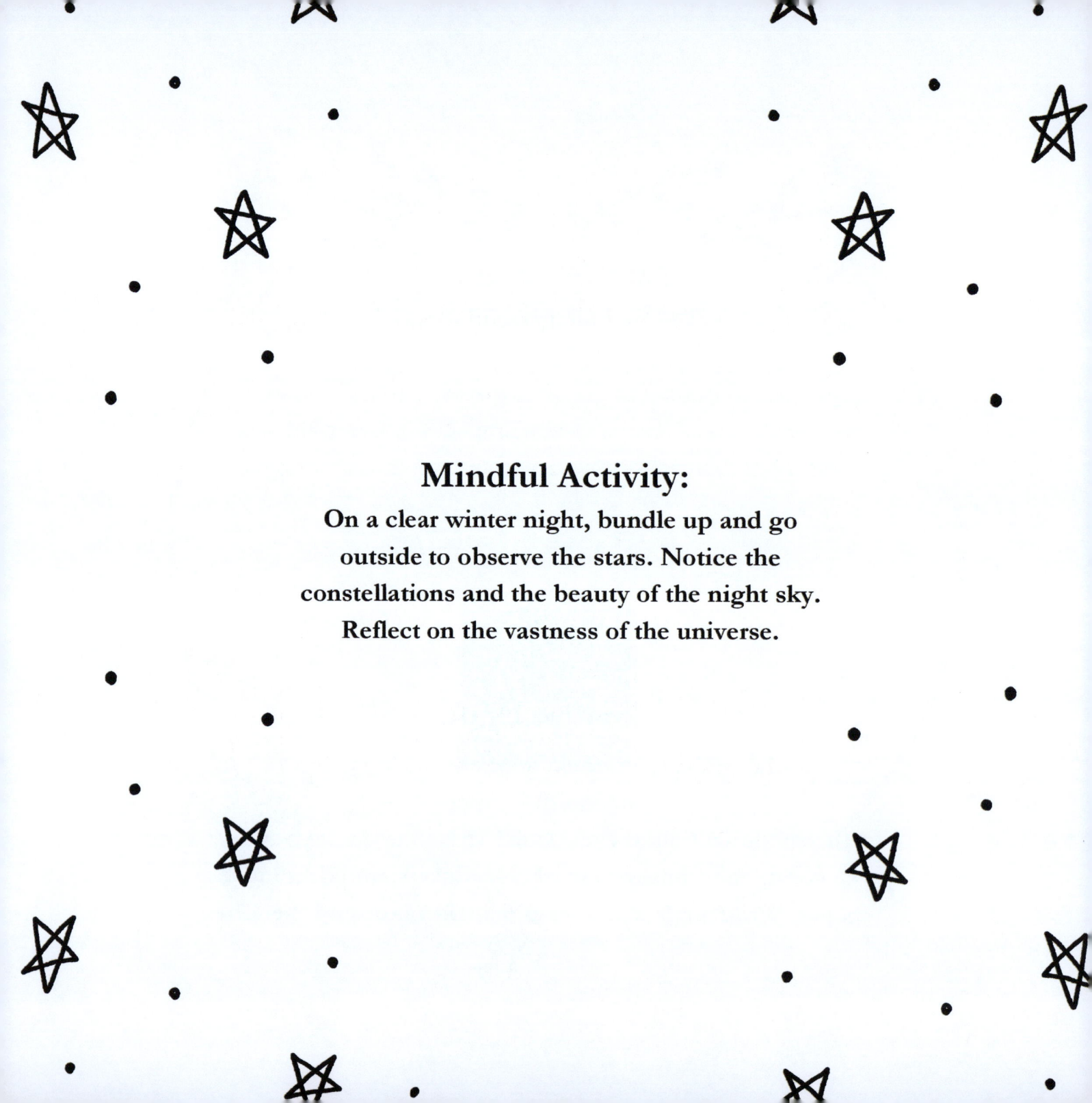

On a clear winter night, bundle up and go outside to observe the stars. Notice the constellations and the beauty of the night sky. Reflect on the vastness of the universe.

Daily Reflection:
Today, I am grateful for...

Mindful Activity:
Learn to identify different types of trees by their bark, shape, and branches. Take a walk and see how many different trees you can identify.

Daily Reflection:
Today, I am grateful for..

Creative Craft:

Materials: Mason jar, water, glycerin, glitter, small figurines, and glue.

Instructions:
Glue the figurine to the inside of the jar lid. Fill the jar with water, add a few drops of glycerin, and sprinkle in glitter. Screw the lid on tightly and shake to see the snow effect.

Daily Reflection:

Today, I am grateful for...

THINGS THAT FILL MY CUP

- TAKING A HOT BATH/SHOWER
- UNDISTURBED READING TIME
- LAUGHING WITH A FRIEND
- TAKING A DAY OFF FOR MYSELF
- WATCHING A SUNRISE
- PLAYING WITH MY KIDS
- GOING FOR A LONG WALK
- LOOKING FORWARD TO A TRIP

Daily Reflection:
Today, I am grateful for..

WINTER
TIP

Breathe easy

Although the air is crisper, don't forget to ventilate your environment daily and breathe in fresh air.

Green Breath Exercise

Find a Natural Spot: If possible, find a spot where you can see some greenery, like a park, garden, or even a plant in your home. If not, simply visualise a lush green landscape.

Inhale: Slowly breathe in through your nose for a count of 4. Imagine you are inhaling the fresh, clean air from the greenery around you.

Hold: Hold your breath for a count of 4. Picture the green energy filling your lungs and spreading throughout your body.

Exhale: Slowly breathe out through your mouth for a count of 4. Visualise any stress or negativity leaving your body with each breath.

Hold: Hold your breath again for a count of 4. Feel the calm and rejuvenation from the green energy.

Repeat: Continue this cycle for 5-10 minutes, or until you feel refreshed and connected to nature.

Tips:

Focus on the colour green and its calming effects.

If your mind wanders, gently bring your attention back to your breath and the green imagery.

Practise this exercise daily to enhance your sense of calm and connection to nature.

Fresh Starts

Reflect on your intentions .
What positive changes do you want to make in your life?

Activity:
Take a walk in nature to clear your mind and set a positive tone for your new beginning. Reflect on your goals and visualise achieving them.

Daily Reflection:
Today, I am grateful for..

Winter Gratitude Meditation

Introduction:
Find a comfortable place to sit or lie down. Close your eyes, take a deep breath, and allow yourself to relax. Let the warmth of your breath soothe you as you settle into this moment of tranquillity.

Breathing and Centring:
Begin by taking slow, deep breaths. Inhale through your nose, filling your lungs completely, and then exhale through your mouth, releasing any tension. Continue to breathe deeply and rhythmically, letting each breath bring you deeper into relaxation.

Visualisation:
Imagine yourself in a serene winter landscape. You are standing at the edge of a peaceful, snow-covered forest. The air is crisp and clear, and the soft, white snow blankets the ground, glistening in the gentle sunlight.

As you breathe in, feel the cool, invigorating air fill your lungs. As you breathe out, imagine your worries and stresses melting away like snowflakes in the sun.

Connection with Nature:
Picture yourself taking a leisurely walk through the forest. With each step, you feel the soft crunch of snow beneath your feet. The trees are adorned with a delicate layer of frost, and the world around you is quiet and still.

Notice the intricate patterns of ice crystals on the branches and the gentle way the snow rests on the evergreen boughs. Take a moment to appreciate the beauty of nature in winter.

Gratitude Reflection:

As you continue your walk, think about the things you are grateful for. Begin with the simple pleasures: the warmth of a cosy blanket, the taste of a comforting hot drink, the joy of a good book.

Gradually expand your gratitude to include the people in your life. Visualise their faces and feel the warmth of their love and support. Reflect on the kindnesses, big and small, that you have experienced and shared.

Embracing Gratitude:

Allow yourself to feel a deep sense of gratitude for all the blessings in your life. Imagine your heart glowing with warmth, like a fire in a cosy cabin. With each breath, let this feeling of gratitude grow stronger and more encompassing.

Say to yourself, either silently or aloud, "I am grateful for the beauty of winter, for the warmth and love in my life, and for the countless blessings that surround me."

Returning to the Present:

Slowly begin to bring your awareness back to the present moment.

Take a few more deep breaths, feeling the rise and fall of your chest.

When you are ready, gently open your eyes. Carry this sense of gratitude with you as you go about your day, remembering the serene winter landscape and the warmth of your heart.

Mindful Activity:

Take a camera or smartphone and go for a walk in nature. Capture the beauty of the winter landscape through photography. Reflect on the unique aspects of the season.

Daily Reflection:
Today, I am grateful for...

Winter Must-Reads

Curl up by the fire, brew a warm drink, and lose yourself in the pages of these enchanting stories:

The Lion, the Witch and the Wardrobe by C.S. Lewis
Step through the wardrobe into the snowy realm of Narnia, where magic and adventure await. A timeless classic perfect for winter's wonder.

A Winter's Tale by Mark Helprin
A beautifully written, magical realism tale set in a glittering New York winter. It's a story of love, hope, and the extraordinary.

The Snow Child by Eowyn Ivey
Inspired by a Russian fairy tale, this novel captures the essence of an Alaskan winter with a story of love, loss, and the magic of belief.

Wintering: The Power of Rest and Retreat in Difficult Times by Katherine May
A reflective, non-fiction book that explores how embracing the quiet and stillness of winter can nurture and transform us.

The Bear and the Nightingale by Katherine Arden
A spellbinding tale steeped in Russian folklore, where winter's frost and ancient spirits come alive in a snowy forest.

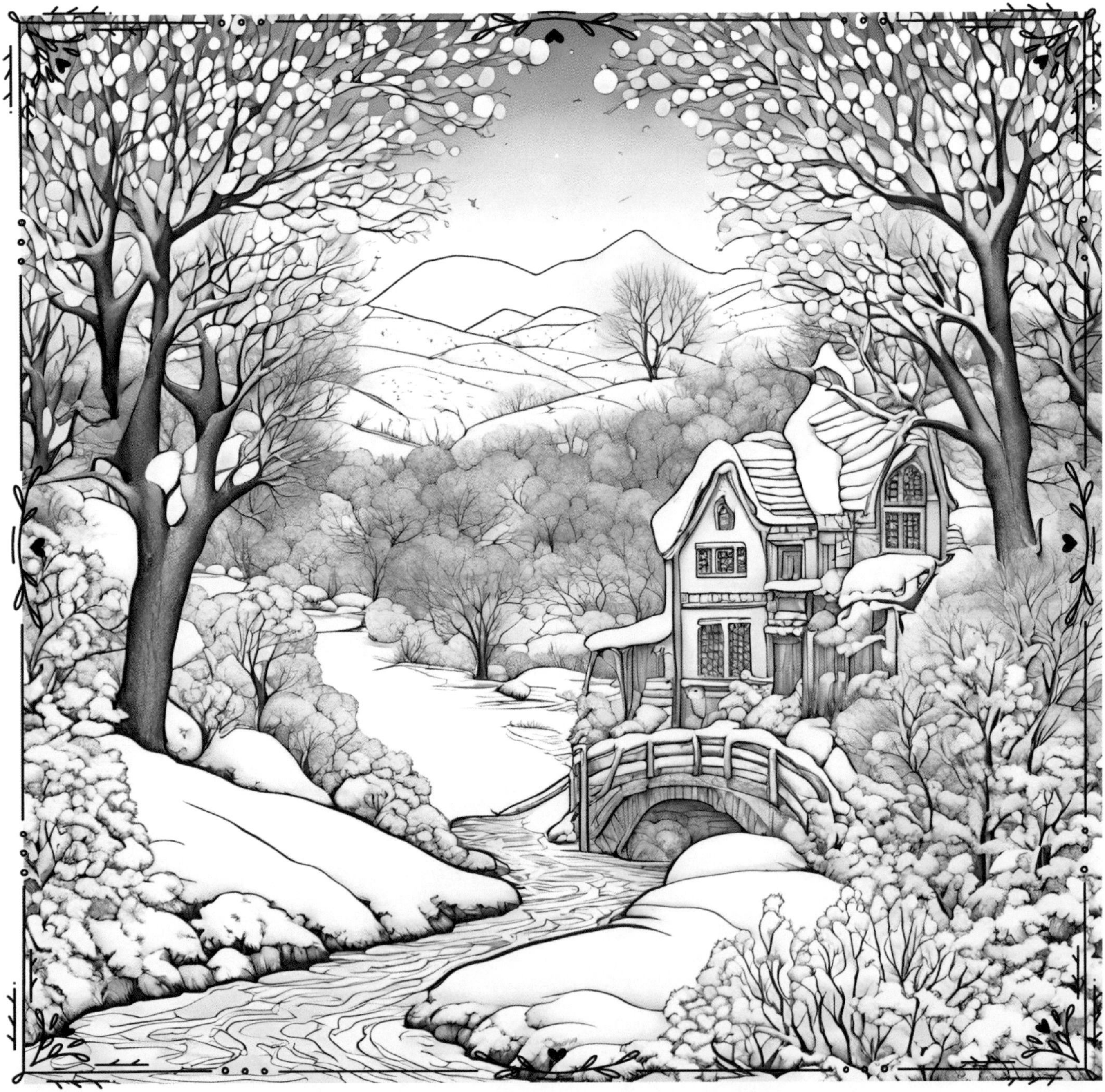

Winter Oats -

Ingredients: Oats, cinnamon, nutmeg, cloves, plant-based milk, and sweetener of choice. you can add fruit, dates and chopped nuts too!

Directions: Cook the oats with plant-based milk and spices for around 5 -7 minutes in a pan on a stove top.
Sweeten to taste and enjoy a warm, nourishing breakfast.

Daily Reflection:

Today, I am grateful for...

Mindful activity-Snowflake Watching

Catch snowflakes on dark fabric and marvel at their intricate designs before they melt.

Daily Reflection:

Today, I am grateful for...

Ice Art Creation

Collect leaves, berries, and petals, arrange them in water-filled containers, and leave them outside to freeze. Admire the frozen art once it's ready.

Daily Reflection:

Today, I am grateful for...

Warming Sweet Potato & Chickpea Stew

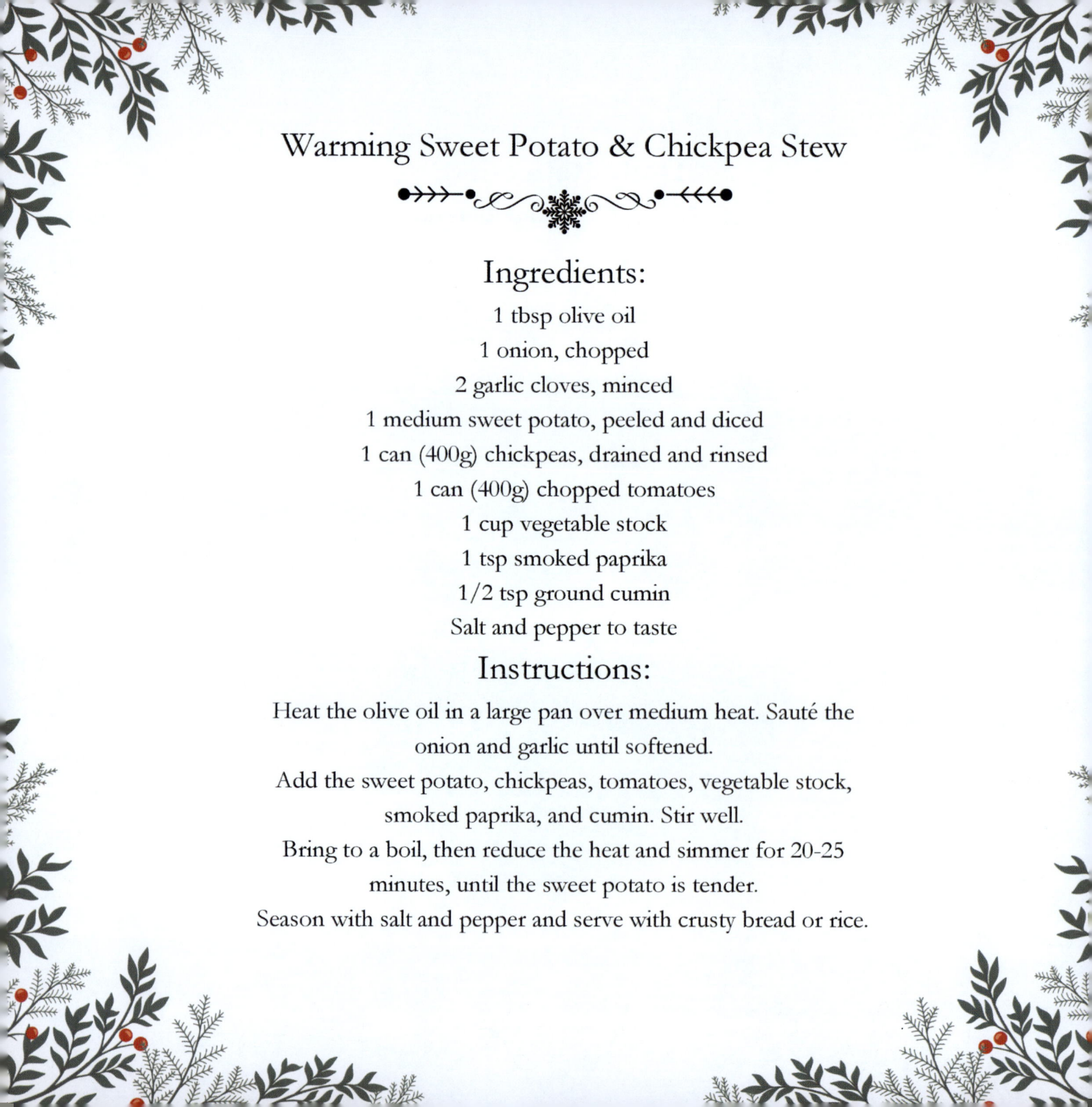

Ingredients:

1 tbsp olive oil
1 onion, chopped
2 garlic cloves, minced
1 medium sweet potato, peeled and diced
1 can (400g) chickpeas, drained and rinsed
1 can (400g) chopped tomatoes
1 cup vegetable stock
1 tsp smoked paprika
1/2 tsp ground cumin
Salt and pepper to taste

Instructions:

Heat the olive oil in a large pan over medium heat. Sauté the onion and garlic until softened.

Add the sweet potato, chickpeas, tomatoes, vegetable stock, smoked paprika, and cumin. Stir well.

Bring to a boil, then reduce the heat and simmer for 20-25 minutes, until the sweet potato is tender.

Season with salt and pepper and serve with crusty bread or rice.

Daily Reflection:

Today, I am grateful for...

Winter Reflection Ritual

Find a quiet moment to reflect on what winter teaches you about stillness, rest, and transformation.

Daily Reflection:
Today, I am grateful for..

Printed in Great Britain
by Amazon